Mental Health & Me

M.J. Anthony

Table of Contents

Introduction...5

What is mental health? 7

   Why is mental health important?..8

   The Benefits of Mental Health..8

Mental Illness 11

   Symptoms 11

   Common Mental Health Issues...12

      Loneliness 12

      Stress 13

      Depression 18

      Anxiety 19

      Post-traumatic Stress Disorder (PTSD) 20

      Bipolar affective disorder 22

      Dissociation and dissociative disorders 23

      Obsessive-compulsive disorder 24

      Paranoia..26

      Psychosis...27

      Schizophrenia 28

   Suicide 29

The Four Basic Emotions 30

   Sadness..31

   Anger 31

   Happiness 32

   Fear...32

Mindfulness 33

   What is Mindfulness? 33

   Benefits of Mindfulness...34

   How to Practice Mindfulness..35

Getting Help..37

   Tips in Getting Help 37

   Professional Treatment 45

Meditation..46

Types of Meditation 48

How to Meditate 52

Positive Thinking..54

A Message for You... 57

Introduction

In September 2017 I fell into a dark spell of depression and anxiety. Over the past three years, I found learning about mental health helped my own journey in understanding my mind.

In our fast-paced and modern world today, many of us are struggling with our mental health. These people may be your family, your neighbors, your friend, your co-worker, or the person sitting beside you on the bus.

However, only a few of these people who struggle with mental health are receiving treatments. The reason for this is the stigma that comes with mental issues. Untreated mental illness might contribute to a higher risk of disorder or higher cost of the medical expenses. This might also result in poor performance and the risk of suicide.

The stigma that comes with mental illness is still powerful as it affects the general view of society with mental health issues. People tend to associate negative stigmas with regards to mental health. Stigmas and misrepresentation are some of the obstacles for someone who is suffering from mental illness.

Mental health is normally overlooked, and this can have a negative effect on the people and the community. And this is where awareness helps. An individual feels devastated and miserable when struggling with anxiety, depression, OCD, and other disorders.

Mental health has also a negative impact on academic success. It is important to encourage emotional support for better well-being. It is about time that society and *us* should help and support those who are suffering from these problems.

Raising awareness is just the beginning of the battle for mental health issues. There is still a lot of work that needs to be done. We should all be aware of it to better understand and to support those who are struggling.

If you are reading this, we hear you. We are here for you. And we support you.

What is mental health?

Mental health is often misunderstood and is frequently used as another term for depression, anxieties, schizophrenia, and many other conditions. Other people view mental health as an illness rather than wellness. The possible reason for this might be associated with the treatment of mental illness or mental health services.

They are connected but not similar. If someone is suffering from mental illness; that does not mean that he/she lacks mental health. The same thing goes if someone lacks mental health; it does not necessarily mean that he/she is suffering from mental illness.

Mental health pertains to our way of thinking, the way we act, and our emotional well-being. It affects our daily way of living especially in our relationships as well as our physical health. It can cope with the normal stresses of life; it can help us to be productive and fruitful and it can shape us to be a better individual that can contribute to the community.

Stress, depression, and anxiety can all affect mental health and interrupt an individual's routine. Maintaining good mental health states our overall well-being. It can preserve our ability to enjoy life and to bring balance to our responsibilities, behaviors, and activities.

Why is mental health important?

An unhealthy mind can affect our physical health. Individuals who are suffering from mental illness are prone to heart disease and heart problems. Poor mental health might cause diabetes, autoimmune skin conditions, osteoporosis, obesity, etc.

Mental health is defined as psychological, social, and emotional well-being. Poor mental health will render us to function less. That being said, poor mental health might also cause mental disorders that will put a huge strain on personal and family relationships and friendship bonds. This can make an individual feel isolated and can worsen their symptoms. So generally, the importance of our mental health is associated with our physical health that is vital to achieving happiness and a better way of living.

When we feel any physical pain, we automatically seek medical attention, but why do we neglect mental illness? The main reason for this is that we set aside mental disorders or illness because we fear that of being talked about or ridiculed or the stigma that is set by the society. Any form of stigma can worsen the problems, especially with mental health.

To overcome this, we must acknowledge the importance of mental health. Being able to talk to someone whom you are comfortable with is a big step in veering away from the stigma. You can reach out to your parents, your siblings, your friend, or your partner. You don't have to be alone. You are not alone. Keep in mind that mental illness is common, and it can be treated. Do not let the stigma stop you from seeking help. We are all in this together.

The Benefits of Mental Health

Intellectual Performance

Having a healthy mind is a promise of a long healthy life span especially in our way of thinking and reasoning. We all aim to be fit and healthy in body and mind. Exercising the mind is the same as how we exercise our bodies. Challenge your mind and acquire new skills. Break out in your comfort zone. You can practice your mental agility by blending in physical movements.

Live Healthy and Longer Life

A fit and healthy mind is correlated to a healthy body. And that will help you live a longer and healthy life. Most of us aim to live physically and mentally healthy until we reach a certain age.

Resilience

Staying mentally healthy will reduce the risk of suffering from mental illness and mental disorders. It will also help us to respond much better to stress. Staying resilient will help us deal with the daily misfortunes of life. We will be more mindful of our physical and mental health.

Being mentally healthy can improve our quality of life. Other benefits of mental health include:

- ✓ Decrease in anxiety
- ✓ Positive moods
- ✓ Clearer thinking
- ✓ Inner peace

- ✓ Improved self-esteem
- ✓ Reduced risk of depression
- ✓ Relationship enhancements
- ✓ Being assertive
- ✓ Good memory
- ✓ Good perception
- ✓ Positive body and physical image
- ✓ Emotionally stable
- ✓ Better well-being
- ✓ Increase in energy

If you are mentally healthy, you have:

- ✓ A sense of contentment
- ✓ A zest for living and the ability to laugh and have fun.
- ✓ The ability to deal with stress and bounce back from adversity.
- ✓ A sense of meaning and purpose, in both their activities and their relationships.
- ✓ The flexibility to learn new skills and adapt to change.
- ✓ A balance between work and play, rest and activity, etc.
- ✓ The ability to build and maintain fulfilling relationships.
- ✓ Self-confidence and high self-esteem.

Mental Illness

Mental illness or mental health a disorder pertains to a wide variety of mental health conditions that can affect our reasoning, thinking, emotions, mood, and behavior. Common examples of mental illness include anxiety disorders, depression, eating disorders, addictive behaviors, and schizophrenia.

Many individuals have mental health issues from time to time. A mental health issue or concern becomes an illness when the on-going signs and symptoms are frequent. This may affect our ability to function less. It can make us feel sad, dejected, and miserable that will also reflect on our relationships, at school, and at work.

Symptoms

The symptoms of mental illness may differ depending on the circumstances and disorder. These signs and symptoms can affect our mood, emotions, thoughts, and behavior that will hinder us from functioning and being productive:

Examples of signs and symptoms include:

- ✓ Sadness, loneliness or feeling down
- ✓ Lack of concentration or focus
- ✓ Excessive fears or worries
- ✓ Extreme feelings of guilt
- ✓ Extreme mood change or being moody
- ✓ Withdrawal from friends and activities
- ✓ Significant tiredness, low energy or problems sleeping

✓ Delusions, paranoia, or hallucinations

✓ Inability to cope with daily problems or stress

✓ Difficulty in understanding and relating to situations and to people

✓ Problems with alcohol or drug use

✓ Major changes in eating habits

✓ Sex drive changes

✓ Excessive anger

✓ Hostility or violence

✓ Suicidal thoughts and tendencies

The symptoms of a mental illness or mental health disorder can sometimes appear as physical problems like back pain, stomach pain, headaches, and other bodily aches and pains.

Common Mental Health Issues

Loneliness

It is a state of distress or a state of discomfort which can result in social disconnection. Even those who are surrounded by others throughout their day, or in a happy relationship, still experience a deep and inescapable loneliness. It is a feeling of lack of connection to the world around you, a feeling like you don't belong and no one understands you.

Loneliness damages men's health with the consequences of social isolation. It is normal for us to feel lonely for some time, but only a few can identify the seriousness of being isolated and lonely. In this modern generation, loneliness is being severed that contributes to violence, substance abuse, and suicide.

It is a feeling of being under pressure and overwhelmed; it is usually experienced when there is an imbalance between what's being asked of us and the ability to deliver or cope with the demands. Stress causes discomfort and uneasiness that can lead other people's mental health problems to anxiety and depression. It can be triggered in any situation including at home, at work, relationship, and other activities. Problems start to arise when you are unable to meet expectations and the coping abilities to deal with the pressure. But stress is a normal feeling.

Two main types of stress:

Acute stress

This type of stress is just short-term as it goes away as fast. You will usually feel it when you have a fight with your partner or a sudden slam on the brake. Stress helps you manage risky circumstances and it also happens when you do something new and exciting. We all experience some point in our life.

Chronic stress

This type of stress lasts for a longer time. You will experience this in situations such as money problems, the pressure at work, and unhappy relationships. If you are experiencing prolonged stress, then that is chronic stress. Sometimes, our mind and body adapt to this kind of situations that we may not notice it is becoming a problem. if you will not manage stress properly, then it might lead to serious health problems.

Our body responds to stress through releasing hormones and these hormones alert our brain more, causes our muscles to tense and increasing our pulse. These responses can help us handle the situation that causes our stress. It is our body's way of protecting itself.

Chronic stress can cause health problems like:

- ✓ High blood pressure
- ✓ Heart disease
- ✓ Diabetes
- ✓ Obesity
- ✓ Depression or anxiety
- ✓ Skin problems, such as acne or eczema
- ✓ Menstrual problems

However, if you have an existing health condition, chronic stress can make it worse.

Signs of stress can be physical and emotional which include the following:

- ✓ Diarrhea or constipation
- ✓ Forgetfulness
- ✓ Frequent aches and pains
- ✓ Headaches
- ✓ Lack of energy or focus
- ✓ Sexual problems
- ✓ Stiff jaw or neck
- ✓ Tiredness

✓ Trouble sleeping or sleeping too much

✓ Upset stomach

✓ Use of alcohol or drugs to relax

✓ Weight loss or gain

Causes of Stress

We react differently to stress. A stressful situation for you might not be stressful for another. Other individuals might trigger stress even in small situations. There is no explanation as to why a person may feel less stressed than the other when faced with the same situation that causes stress. For some, mental health issues like anxiety and depression can trigger other people more easily than others.

Common situations that can trigger stress:

✓ job issues or retirement

✓ lack of time or money

✓ bereavement

✓ family problems

✓ illness

✓ moving home

✓ relationships, marriage, and divorce

Other issues include:

✓ abortion or pregnancy loss

✓ driving in heavy traffic or fear of an accident

✓ fear of crime or problems with neighbors

✓ pregnancy and becoming a parent

✓ excessive noise, overcrowding, and pollution

✓ uncertainty or waiting for an important outcome

Some individuals who experience traumatic or tragic event are suffering from stress. This is called PTSD or post-traumatic stress disorder.

The physical effects of stress can include:

✓ sweating

✓ pain in the back or chest

✓ cramps or muscle spasms

✓ fainting

✓ headaches

✓ nervous twitches

✓ pins and needles sensations

Emotional reactions can include:

✓ anger

✓ burnout

✓ concentration issues

✓ fatigue

✓ a feeling of insecurity

✓ forgetfulness

✓ irritability

✓ nail biting

✓ restlessness

✓ sadness

Stress-associated behaviors include:

- ✓ food cravings and eating too much or too little
- ✓ sudden angry outbursts
- ✓ drug and alcohol misuse
- ✓ higher tobacco consumption
- ✓ social withdrawal
- ✓ frequent crying
- ✓ relationship problems

Chronic stress can lead to several complications like:

- ✓ anxiety
- ✓ depression
- ✓ heart disease
- ✓ high blood pressure
- ✓ lower immunity against diseases
- ✓ muscular aches
- ✓ PTSD
- ✓ sleeping difficulties
- ✓ indigestion
- ✓ impotence and loss of libido

It is an intense feeling of sadness that can last for a long time. Depression is a mood disorder that causes a loss of interest and can interfere with your daily life function. This is a common and serious medical illness that can affect us negatively.

But good news, this mood disorder is treatable. Depression will affect the activities that we enjoy. We lose interest in the things we do if we suffer from depression. It can also lead to different emotional and physical complications. Symptoms of depression include:

- ✓ Feeling sad or having a depressed mood
- ✓ Loss of interest or pleasure in activities once enjoyed
- ✓ Changes in appetite or weight loss
- ✓ Irregular sleeping habit
- ✓ Loss of energy or increased fatigue
- ✓ Feeling worthless or guilty
- ✓ Difficulty thinking, concentrating or making decisions
- ✓ Thoughts of death or suicide

If these symptoms will last for two weeks, then it can be diagnosed as depression. Other medical conditions have similar symptoms as depression such as brain tumors, thyroid problems, and vitamin deficiency. So, it is important to rule out medical causes.

Depression over Sadness over Grief

The feeling of sadness and grief is normal for unfortunate situations like losing a job, break up from a relationship, and the death of a loved one. Sometimes those who experienced loss might define what they feel like depression. However, being sad is not the same as depression. Sadness is a symptom of depression.

Anxiety

I was diagnosed with Generlized Anxiety Disorder in 2017. It is a consistent state of extreme worry or fear about perceived threats, which is usually out of proportion to the reality of the situation which can be mild or severe. Anxiety can happen without any specific reason or cause. It can be a major impact on physical and mental health.

We all experience anxiety from time to time. When we are in a situation that we are not used to, anxiety kicks in. You are suffering from anxiety if you feel ill-tempered, worried, easily irritated, insecure and extreme loneliness. A low level of anxiety is good but too much of it may indicate a serious issue.

Recurring anxiety attacks may be bad and could progress into Generalized Anxiety Disorder (GAD) and depression. Anxiety can also stop us from doing what we want and achieving our goals.

Anxiety can happen to anyone. It can also be triggered in a tiny amount of inconvenience. Frequent anxiety attacks will lead to abnormal cases. Fears and stress are the biggest influences on higher levels of anxiety.

Like stress, anxiety is also a normal emotion we feel when we face problems, loneliness, and personal issues. But there are specific levels of anxiety that needs to be observed.

Normal Anxiety

Normal anxiety happens when the anxiousness level matches the magnitude of the situation. Anxiety attack has minimal effect on an individual's life and these attacks happen very occasionally. It is usually caused by the feeling of regrets, remembering certain memories, and not achieving a specific task.

Abnormal Anxiety

Generalized Anxiety Disorder (GAD), panic attacks, PSTD, etc. fall under abnormal anxiety. The anxiety level with abnormal anxiety is out of proportion when matched with the magnitude of the situation which can trigger an attack. If you think you are suffering from the mentioned symptoms, then it will be better if you seek professional help.

Be wary of our mental health and have regular consultations or regular mental exercises. If you think you have the symptoms of an underlying mental health disorder, talk to your doctor or a professional before you suffer from serious consequences.

Post-traumatic Stress Disorder (PTSD)

Post-traumatic stress disorder is a mental health condition that can develop as a response to people who have experienced any traumatic event. These traumatic events may be a serious accident, war-related events, or torture, physical or sexual assault, or natural disasters such as bushfires or floods. People who are suffering from this disorder are distrustful and always on guard, they also have terrifying nightmares, they feel emotionally numb and detached.

Individuals who experience such unfortunate events will have reactions like anger, shock, fear, nervousness, and even guilt. These reactions are common and normal. But when an individual suffers from PSTD, these reactions may continue to become strong that they will keep an individual from living a normal life.

Symptoms of PSTD:

Reliving

PTSD will recurrently recall the suffering through thoughts and recollections of the trauma. Flashbacks, hallucinations, and nightmares will repeatedly occur when a person is suffering from PSTD. A particular date of the unfortunate event can also cause the trauma that may lead to distress.

Avoiding

An individual will avoid the places, people, thoughts or anything that is related and that could remind him/her of the trauma. This can result in isolation and detachment from family and friends.

Increased arousal

This symptom of PSTD includes extreme emotions like feeling or showing affection, problems relating to others, sleep irregularities, outbursts of anger, irritability, difficulty concentrating and being jumpy. There are also physical symptoms like rapid breathing, muscle tension, diarrhea, nausea and increased blood pressure and heart rate.

Negative Thoughts and Mood

This symptom is related to memories of the tragic event and is related to blame.

It is a type of mood disorder, previously referred to as 'manic depression'. A person with bipolar disorder experiences episodes of the feeling of being elated and depressed. The cause of this is unknown and the person may or may not experience psychotic symptoms. Environmental stressors can trigger episodes of this mental issue.

Bipolar disorder is a long-term condition. However, you can manage your mood swings and other symptoms if you will follow a treatment plan. Bipolar disorder is usually treated with medications and psychotherapy or psychological counseling.

Symptoms of bipolar affective disorder:

- ✓ Jumpy or wired
- ✓ Hyperactive
- ✓ Feeling of euphoria
- ✓ Decreased need for sleep
- ✓ Unusual talkativeness
- ✓ Racing thoughts
- ✓ Distractibility
- ✓ Poor decision-making
- ✓ Major depressive episode
- ✓ Feeling sad and empty
- ✓ Hopelessness
- ✓ Loses interest in other activities
- ✓ Weight loss
- ✓ Weight gain

- ✓ Sleeping irregularities

- ✓ Strange behavior

- ✓ Fatigue or exhausted

- ✓ Feelings of worthlessness

- ✓ Lack of concentration

- ✓ Suicidal thoughts

Dissociation and dissociative disorders

This is a mental process where a person disconnects from their thoughts, feelings, memories, or sense of identity. These disorders include dissociative amnesia, depersonalization disorder, dissociative fugue, and dissociative identity disorder.

Common Dissociation Symptoms

- ✓ Daydreaming, spacing out, or eyes glazed over

- ✓ Acting differently or acting strangely

- ✓ Sudden change in emotions or reactions

Signs of a Dissociative Disorder

- ✓ Amnesia

- ✓ Memory loss

- ✓ Depersonalization

- ✓ Identity Disorder

Obsessive-compulsive disorder (OCD) is an anxiety disorder where they have recurrent thoughts, images or impulses that are intrusive and unwanted. These obsessions and compulsions affect daily life activities and cause distress.

Obsessions

These are disturbing thoughts or urges that repeatedly happen. Individuals with OCD are trying to conquer these urges but something in them knows that somehow the thoughts might be true.

Symptoms:

- ✓ Fear of contamination or dirt
- ✓ Doubting and having difficulty tolerating uncertainty
- ✓ Needing things orderly and symmetrical
- ✓ Aggressive or horrific thoughts about losing control and harming yourself or others
- ✓ Unwanted thoughts, including aggression, or sexual or religious subjects

Examples include:

- ✓ Fear of being contaminated by touching objects that other people have touched
- ✓ Doubtful like if you have locked the door or turned off the stove
- ✓ When objects aren't orderly or facing a certain way and you will feel intense stress

✓ Thinking of shouting obscenities or curses

✓ Acting inappropriately in public

✓ Prohibited sexual images

✓ Avoidance of situations that can trigger obsessions

Compulsions

Opposite to obsession, compulsions are repetitive acts. Compulsion acts as a reliever to stress and anxiety caused by obsession.

Symptoms:

✓ Washing and cleaning

✓ Checking

✓ Counting

✓ Orderliness

✓ Following a strict routine

✓ Demanding reassurance

Examples of compulsions:

✓ Hand-washing until your skin becomes raw

✓ Checking doors repeatedly to make sure they're locked

✓ Checking the stove repeatedly to make sure it's off

✓ Counting in certain patterns

✓ Silently repeating a prayer, word or phrase

✓ Arranging your canned goods to face the same way

It is the irrational and persistent feeling of unrealistic distrust and being persecuted. Paranoia may be a symptom of conditions including paranoid personality disorder and schizophrenia.

Symptoms of paranoia:

- ✓ constant stress or anxiety related to beliefs they have about others
- ✓ mistrust of others
- ✓ feeling disbelieved or misunderstood
- ✓ feeling victimized or persecuted when there isn't a threat
- ✓ isolation

Paranoid schizophrenia is a mental illness which refers to an individual who can be distrustful and suspicious of other people. They always seem guarded and they also have delusions or they believe that others will hurt them.

Causes of paranoia

It is not fully comprehensible as to why some of us develop personality disorders or mental illness. This may be because of these factors:

- ✓ genetics
- ✓ stress
- ✓ brain chemistry

Other conditions of paranoia are:

- ✓ bipolar disorder
- ✓ anxiety
- ✓ depression

Psychosis

It is a condition that will make the person experience delusions, hallucinations, and confused thinking. It will cause the person to lose touch with reality. It is also a symptom and not an illness. The causes of this condition are mental or physical illness, substance abuse, or extreme stress or trauma.

Symptoms of psychosis include:

- ✓ difficulty concentrating
- ✓ depressed mood
- ✓ sleeping too much or not enough
- ✓ anxiety
- ✓ suspiciousness
- ✓ withdrawal from family and friends
- ✓ delusions
- ✓ hallucinations
- ✓ disorganized speech, such as switching topics erratically
- ✓ depression
- ✓ suicidal thoughts or actions

Causes of psychosis

Illnesses that can cause psychosis include:

- ✓ brain diseases such as Parkinson's disease, Huntington's disease, and some chromosomal disorders
- ✓ brain tumors or cysts

Dementia may result in psychosis caused by:

- ✓ Alzheimer's disease
- ✓ HIV
- ✓ Syphilis
- ✓ Other infections that attack the brain
- ✓ some types of epilepsy
- ✓ stroke

Schizophrenia

It is a complex psychotic disorder in which people interpret reality abnormally. Hallucinations, delusions, thought disorder, social withdrawal, lack of motivation, and impaired thinking and memory are some of the symptoms. This disorder has a high risk of suicide.

In regards to the number of factors including social norms, upbringing and the role models we recognized with, men's mental health issues have been unrecognized for a long time.

Suicide

Suicide is mostly associated with depression, physical pain and illness, loneliness, hopelessness, and sometimes guilt.

Suicide means intentionally ending your own life. People who experience suicidal thoughts and feelings are suffering most often from depression or other mental illness.

Suicide affects all people and we were all shocked when a famous celebrated TV chef and world traveler like Anthony Bourdain took his own life. He was an image of success and satisfaction. Apparently, behind the glamorous surface is a dark deep end. His death made us realized how little we addressed male suicide.

A common gender stereotype is that men are emotionally disconnected and uninterested in showing any feelings. It is viewed as a sign of weakness and because of this, men typically avoid the mental health support systems.

Common risk factors for suicide are:

- Social isolation or living alone
- Not being able to form or sustain meaningful relationships
- Divorce or relationship breakdowns
- A history of physical and sexual abuse
- Imprisonment
- Being bullied at school, college, or work
- Unemployment
- Loss of a loved one through trauma or disease
- Mental illness, particularly where this is related to depression and painful or debilitating illnesses or conditions

What are the risk factors?

- Difficulties accessing or receiving care
- Access to means of suicide
- Inappropriate media reporting
- The stigma associated with mental health, substance abuse
- Poverty
- Experiences of trauma or abuse
- Experiences of disaster, war, or conflict
- Experiences of discrimination
- Isolation and lack of social support
- Relationship breakdown
- Loss or conflict
- Previous suicide attempts
- Financial loss
- Chronic pain
- Family history of suicide

The Four Basic Emotions

Sadness

Sadness is perhaps the most know negative emotion of a person and often seen as the opposite of happiness. Everything we gain in life will eventually have to lose it. A person can feel sad whenever he loses something important. The loss can take place in many ways, depending on the thing that is lost. The loss might be irreparably damaged, cease, vanish, pass away, decrease or irreversibly change.

Material possessions like losing your favorite shoes, losing money, and a relationship like going through a breakup contribute to daily sadness.
A person who is sad essentially tries to deal with the loss and accommodates life without the cherished or important thing. The duration of a person to feel this emotion depends on the weight of the loss. Sad people frequently have the urge to stop their daily activities and will take time to reflect on the situation.

Anger

Anger is an emotion that links to hatred or resentment toward someone or something you feel have intentionally done something wrong to you. It is a powerful emotion that will command you to fight due to the intensity of what you feel. Anger an intense negative emotion that will range from mild irritation to rage. The prolonged release of the stress that coheres with anger can destroy neurons in areas of the brain related to judgment and short-term memory, and this can weaken the immune system.

Happiness

Happiness is the feeling of satisfaction, fulfillment, appreciation of life, and moments of pleasure, but overall, it has to do with the positive experience of emotions. It is a feeling of contentment. A person can feel perfect happiness when all of the needs are being met and satisfied.

Happiness is considered the most acceptable in society with these four emotions, though fear, anger, and sadness are generally felt by everyone. These emotions help valued the purposes in our lives and these are normal responses to threat and loss.

Fear

Fear is a powerful, natural, and primitive emotion. Fear alerts a person the presence of danger or the threat of harm, whether that danger is physical or psychological. It also comprises a universal biochemical response as to a high individual emotional response.

Fear stems from real threats and danger and it can also be a symptom of some mental health conditions including panic disorder, social anxiety disorder, phobias, and post-traumatic stress disorder (PTSD).

People might not always be able to identify what they are feeling or have the words to describe their emotions. But sometimes, we just need a helping hand and listening ears to let the person know that he/she is not alone.

Mindfulness

What is Mindfulness?

Mindfulness is maintaining a moment by moment awareness of your thoughts, feelings, body sensations, and the environment that surrounds you through a gentle and nurturing lens. It involves acceptance which means paying attention to your thoughts without judging them but believing them. Mindfulness will tune your thoughts to sensing the present moment rather than rehashing the past or imagining the future.

This simply means "being present" and giving your full attention to the moment that you are in and that you are aware of where you are and what you are doing. Mindfulness is a close relative of meditation but they differ in some important ways that make it much more accessible to people. Compare to meditation, mindfulness is less intensive and it's easier to achieve. Mindfulness does not aim to quiet your mind but the goal of it is to become aware of the inner work of your mental, physical, and emotional process that you easily take for granted.

The best way to understood self-awareness is through mindfulness. It will help you acknowledge, accept, and deal with difficult thoughts and emotions.

Mindfulness helps you set a space between yourselves and your impulsive reactions that can help you identify and change your condition and automatic responses. It will help you learn to focus on your attention. It has been long adapted and used in treatment for depression especially for preventing relapses and for assisting with mood regulation and anger management issues.

The state of dwelling on painful memories, problems, worries, and fears about the future which are similar to anxiety and depression reduces the rumination through the help of mindfulness. It creates an anchor to the present that will stop your mind from getting stressed and overwhelmed.

Benefits of Mindfulness

- It will help you sleep better
- Reduce chronic pain
- Relieve stress
- Fight off depression
- You will become more compassionate
- Get sick less often
- Increase in focus
- Improve performance
- Control emotions such as impatience, anger and fear
- Enhance relationships
- Build emotional intelligence

How to Practice Mindfulness

Mindfulness has two parts: learning to focus your attention and bringing you attention back when it wanders then learning to be open without the judgment and curious about what you bring your focus to. It is easy and accessible to practice. You can practice just by yourself or with your friends.

Focus on Five Senses:

Focus on the five senses—touch, taste, smell, sight and hearing. As you return your focus from your five senses, it returns you to the present and decreases your anxiety and stress. Here are five steps to help you focus on your senses:

Look around your environment. Be aware of your surroundings. Notice five things you would not normally see.

Now notice four things you can feel such as your clothes against your skin or the smoothness of the cup as you drink your coffee.

Next notice three things you can hear. What noises are in the background? Do you hear a barking dog in the distance or the humming of the refrigerator in the kitchen?

Now, what can you smell? The smell of a barbecue your neighbors are cooking or freshly mown grass. Notice one thing you can taste; the taste of freshly brewed coffee or the taste in your mouth.

How to start:
- Set your timer to 5 minutes

- You can sit or stand quietly
- Then pay attention to the present moment, without judgment.
- Focus on your senses: your sense of smell, taste, touch, sense of hearing, and what you see. Just analyze and don't think too much.

If disturbing thoughts will start to enter your mind, just simply note them and bring your attention and focus on your senses again. If you want to calm your mind from racing, breathe in and out calmly and focus on your breath to slow down your thoughts.
The more you do it the more gets easier. You can also incorporate it with your daily routine like your house chores.

However, it may be often recommended for people dealing with mental and emotional issues, this practice can be harmful in some cases and can lead to anxiety, panic, and re-experiencing traumatic memories. If a person suffers from serious mental health problems like schizophrenia or bipolar disorder, it should consult with a professional first before undergoing intensive mindfulness practice
Mindfulness may not work for everyone, and it doesn't work after several times of trying, stop it and try something else.

Getting Help

Please do not try to fight out mental illness on your own. It might take courage to seek help from the family, loved ones, or a professional, but please do not hesitate. An individual with mental illness responds well to self-step such as reaching out for social support, exercising, switching to a healthy diet, and making other lifestyle changes. But do not expect your mood to lighten instantly. You will likely begin to feel a little better each day.

A lot of us that recovers from mental illness will notice improvements in sleep patterns and appetite before improvements in their mood. But these steps can have a controlling effect on how you think and feel, that will help you overcome the symptoms of mental illness and regain your enjoyment of life.

Tips in Getting Help

Seek social support

Hectic schedules and work commitments are often the factors that make it difficult for us to find time to maintain friendships and a relationship. However, the first step to undertake mental illness is to find people that you can connect with. It doesn't simply mean trading jokes with a coworker or chatting about the weather and sports with the person sitting next to you in a bar.

It basically means finding someone that you feel comfortable sharing your feelings with and what goes on your mind. Find someone who will listen to you without judgment and telling you how you should feel or think.

People might think that discussing their feelings with someone is embarrassing. If you are short-tempered, drinking a lot than your usual, or worst punching a hole in your wall, these are the closest things you will know that something is not right. Opting to talk about what you are feeling and what you are going through can actually help you feel better.

Find social support to fight depression. For people who are suffering from depression, reaching out to other people can seem overwhelming. But, developing and maintaining a close relationship is essential to help you get through the dark and tough times. If you feel like you don't have anyone to turn to, guys, it is never too late to build new friendships and improve your support network.

Look for support from someone who makes you feel safe and cared for. This person you talk to won't fix you but that person would be there to listen. Find a good listener that who will listen to you attentively and compassionately without judging you.

Social media, text messaging, phone calls are good ways to stay in touch. But do not replace the person-to-person quality time with those. That simple face-to-face or personal chat will make you feel relieved and will keep away depression.

Be active or indulge in social activities even if sometimes you don't feel like it. When a person is depressed, nothing is more comfortable than staying with your shell. But, if you are surrounded by people, you will feel less depressed.

Find ways to support other people. It will be nice to receive support from others but studies show that if you provide support, your mood will improve. Do volunteer works, listen to a friend, and do something nice and good for somebody.

Adopt and care for a pet. Nothing beats a human connection; however, pets can bring joy and companionship in your life and will make you feel less isolated. This will also give you a sense of being needed which is a good antidote to depression.

Join a support group. Being with other people with the same dilemma as yours can go a long way in reducing your sense of isolation. You can either encourage each other and give and take advice on how to cope. Sharing your experiences is a good way to release that negative feeling.

Invite someone to a night out, movie, or concert. There are plenty of other people who feel just as awkward about reaching out and making friends as you do.

Break the ice and invite someone to go shopping or watch a ballgame with you. Reach out and have fun. Reconnect with your old pals, even if you haven't been seeing each other and talking to each other for a long time, exerting an effort is a good way to reconnect.

Support your health

Having a positive lifestyle change can help a person deal with mental illness to keep it from coming back.

Have a good 8 hours of sleep if you can. Depression mostly involves sleep problems. You might be sleeping too much or too little, but this will make your mood suffer.

Keep that little annoying stress in check. Not only it will worsen and prolong your depression, but stress can also trigger it. Find out all the things in your life that stress you out, and find ways to relieve them.

Do relaxation techniques. A daily relaxation routine can help you relieve and fight off symptoms of depression, reduce stress, and boss the feeling of joy and your well-being. You can do yoga, deep breathing exercises, and meditation.

Get outside once in a while. Good sunlight will do you good. Exposing yourself to the sun will help boost serotonin levels that will improve your mood. You can take a walk, drink your morning coffee outside, take out your pet, and do your exercises in the yard.

Have a list of things that you can do to boost your mood. Like the list below:

- Spend some time in nature
- List what you like about yourself
- Read a good book
- Watch a funny movie or TV show
- Take a long, hot shower
- Take care of a few small tasks
- Play with a pet (*I have four cats and they help on bad days*)
- Talk to friends or family face-to-face
- Listen to music
- Do something spontaneous

Do Exercises

If you are depressed, getting out of bed seems like a discouraging thing to do, let alone working out. But exercise is a powerful depression beater and one of the most important tools in your recovery box. Studies show that doing regular exercise can be effective in relieving the symptoms of depression. It will also prevent an episode of relapses.

You only need at least 30 minutes of your time to exercise each day. You can start small movements. A regular 10-minute-walk outside can also improve your mood.

Getting up to exercise is difficult especially if you are depressed and you feel exhausted. But research shows that the level of your energy will improve if you keep up with it. it will keep your energized and will lessen fatigue. Search for exercises that are rhythmic and continuous movements. Most exercises are walking, weight training, swimming, or martial arts-where you move both your arms and legs.

Find an exercise partner. Working out with someone will enable you to spend time socializing and will keep you motivated. You can also join a running club, enrolling in a gym or another sports league.

Tips to start your exercise routine

- The goal for 30 minutes of your routine activity on most days. To make it easier, you can cut out the 30 minutes to 3 sessions by doing 10-minute each a day. You can start with walking or dancing.
- Do exercise with blended movements engaging both your arms and legs like running, swimming, walking, martial arts, dancing and weight training.
- You can incorporate mindfulness on your workouts. Just focus on how your body feels rather than your thoughts.
- Stick to your workout.

Eat Healthily

If you love sugar and carbs, well, it's it to minimize on your favorites. Your favorites goodies like pasta, fries, baked goods, and sugary snacks will quickly lead to crash your mood and energy.

Foods that can adversely affect your moods, such as caffeine, alcohol, trans fats. If you like food with high levels of chemical preservatives or hormones then you need to be careful and only take minimal servings.

Eat a lot of food with Omega-3 fatty acids to give your mood a boost. The best foods with Omega-3 fatty acids are fish, seaweeds, flaxseed, and walnuts.

Eat foods with mood-enhancing nutrients, such as bananas and spinach. Avoid foods with deficiencies in B vitamins which can trigger depression and eat a lot of citrus fruit, leafy greens, beans, chicken, and eggs

Foods that adversely affect mood:

- Caffeine
- Alcohol
- Trans fats
- High levels of chemical preservatives
- Sugary snacks
- Refined carbs
- Fried food

Foods that boost mood

- Fatty fish rich in Omega-3s such as salmon, herring, mackerel, anchovies, sardines, tuna
- Nuts such as walnuts, almonds, cashews, peanuts
- Avocados
- Flaxseed
- Beans

- Leafy greens such as spinach, kale, Brussel's sprouts

- Fresh fruit such as blueberries

Fight off Negative Thinking

Depression sets a negative turn on everything, including the way you see yourself and your hopes for the future.

When negatives thoughts overwhelm you, remember that this is a symptom of your depression and these irrational, pessimistic attitudes are not realistic. You cannot break out of this negativity by telling yourself to just think positive. It became a lifelong pattern of thinking that has become so automatic and you are not even completely aware of it. The secret is to identify these negative thoughts that fuel your depression and replace them with a more balanced way of thinking.

Negative ways of thinking that fuel depression:

- All-or-nothing thinking or thinking of being a total failure.
- Overgeneralization or thinking that you cannot do anything right.
- Mental filter or ignoring the positive things and you only focus on the negative. You only notice those things that went wrong rather than noticing the things that went right.
- Lessening the positive or thinking up and coming up with reasons to mask the positive to negative.
- Jumping to conclusions or making negative interpretations without the actual evidence.
- Emotional reasoning or believing that the way you feel reflects reality.
- Labeling or classifying yourself based on your mistakes and shortcomings.

Professional Treatment

When is the time to ask for help?

If you're worried that someone you care about may be struggling, or you think that you yourself need help, look for these signs that indicate a need for outside assistance:

- Change in mood
- The difference in work performance
- Weight changes
- Sadness, hopelessness, or pulling away from things that used to provide enjoyment
- Physical symptoms, such as headaches and stomach issues

If you recognize any of these symptoms in your loved one or a friend, remind them that asking for help is a sign of strength and not a weakness.

To treat this problem, we must get the message across that it's OK to ask for help, whether for yourself, your loved ones, or anyone you think may need it.

And if you are someone you that had overcome a mental health problem, do not be afraid to share your stories. Reducing the stigma means you are willing to talk about the times you have needed to ask for help ourselves.

And if the support coming from family and friends and positive lifestyle changes are not enough, seek help from a professional. Open up about how you feel together with your physical symptoms.

Treatments include:

Therapy

A person may feel that talking to a stranger about his/her problems is uncomfortable. However, if therapy is available to you, it can often bring a swift sense of relief, even to the most skeptical person.

Medication

Antidepressant medication can help relieve some symptoms of depression, but it doesn't cure the underlying problem and is rarely a long-term solution. The medication also comes with side effects. Yes, medication is a big help and the right way to approach the mental health issues, but you can always follow self-help as well. Therapy and lifestyle changes can address the underlying causes of your depression to prevent it from returning when you're able to come off antidepressants.

Meditation

Meditation changes your brain and the way your body responds to stress. It works wonderfully on depression, stress, anxiety, and post-traumatic stress disorder. Studies and research suggest that meditation can bring health benefits, especially on mental health.

It isn't about becoming a whole new different person or will make you even a better person because it is about training in awareness and getting a healthy sense of perspective. You are not trying to turn off your thoughts or feelings; rather, you are learning to observe them without judgment. And in due time, you may start to better understand them as well.

Meditation is also like learning any other skill. Just think of it like when you do some exercises for your muscles that you've been working on for the first time. It takes consistent practice to get comfortable. And it's usually easier if you have a teacher. We've got you covered there.

There's no such thing as perfect meditation. Your focus might wander, and you will forget to follow your breath. And that is okay. It's part of the experience. What's most important is to meditate consistently. It's one of those things where the journey is more important than the destination.

It takes time to get comfortable with your mind. There might be setbacks along the way but that's part of meditating. Keep practicing because you are doing great just by showing up.

When we sit to meditate, we are looking after ourselves in ways that might not at first seem obvious. Meditation has a lot of benefits which are supported by science. Many people start meditating to manage stress, reduce anxiety, and to cultivate peace of mind. But there are thousands of studies documenting other less-known mindfulness meditation benefits, which can have a positive impact on mental, physical, and emotional health. Read on to find out more about the many health benefits of meditation you may experience when you establish a practice and repeat it consistently.

Types of Meditation

Guided and unguided meditation

The first step to start a medication is choosing between guided and unguided meditation. Practicing guided meditation, a teacher or instructor will guide you through the basic steps of the practice. This type of meditation is particularly useful for beginners because the teacher is experienced and trusted, and their guidance can be the key to helping those who are new to medication that get the most out of the experience.

Guided meditation explains how the mind behaves throughout meditation that will lead you through a specific meditation technique, and then it suggests how to integrate this technique into your everyday life.

In unguided meditation, which is also called silent meditation, you meditate alone, without someone else explaining the process. For some individuals, unguided meditation includes simply sitting in quiet and paying attention to the body and thoughts for a set period of time.

Calming and insight meditation

Meditation techniques are mostly described as calming or insight meditation. Calming meditation aims to cultivate a quieter, more peaceful state of mind and improved concentration. Calming meditation involves focusing on a particular object like your breath, a mantra, visualization, a physical object, even physical sensations within your body, and returning to that object whenever you get preoccupied or distracted and you notice your mind starting to wander.

On the other hand, people who do insight meditation often set an intention to change their minds by evolving qualities such as wisdom and compassion. Insight meditation pertains to focusing on the breath and being aware of and noting all the physical and mental sensations that arise.

The interesting fact about meditation is that it doesn't have to be one or the other, calming or insight. In fact, many meditation techniques actually combine elements of both. To help us find calmness and inner peace of mind, these meditations also help improve feelings of well-being, happiness, and empathy for others.

Zen meditation

This ancient and traditional meditation includes sitting upright and following the breath, particularly the way it moves in and out of the belly and letting the mind wander. This meditation aims to foster a sense of presence alertness.

Mantra meditation

This type of medication is similar to focused attention meditation, although instead of focusing on the breath to quiet the mind, you focus on a mantra which could be a syllable, word, or phrase. The idea here is that the subtle vibrations associated with the repeated mantra can encourage positive change or maybe a boost in self-confidence or increased compassion for others and can help you enter an even deeper state of meditation.

Transcendental meditation

This type of meditation includes sitting comfortably with one's eyes closed for 20 minutes twice per day and engaging in the effortless practice as instructed. Students are encouraged to practice twice a day, which often includes morning meditation, and a second session is in the mid-afternoon or early evening.

Yoga meditation

There are a lot of types of meditation that has the same style as yoga, particularly Kundalini yoga. This type of mediation aims at strengthening the nervous system, so we are better able to cope with everyday stress and problems. However, in order to integrate the neuromuscular changes that happen during yoga and gain the greatest benefit from the practice, we must take time for **savasana** or **Shavasana** (or the corpse or relaxation pose) to relax the body and release tension.

Vipassana meditation

Vipassana is another ancient mediation that invites you to use your concentration to intensely examine certain aspects of your existence with the intention of eventual transformation. This type of mediation pushes us to find insight into the true nature of reality, thru the contemplation of several key areas of human existence: "suffering, not being satisfied," "impermanence," "non-self," and "emptiness."

Chakra meditation

This meditation technique is aimed at keeping the body's core chakras or the centers of energy which is open, aligned, and fluid. Blocked or imbalanced chakras can result in uncomfortable physical and mental symptoms, but chakra meditation can help to bring all of them back into balance.

How to Meditate

Life is pretty simple. Most of everything we want in life like more love, freedom, success, or chocolate requires that we have clarity. Specifically, clarity about what we want. Meditation provides a lot of benefits, but for this situation, it will strengthen your ability to be present and eradicate all the negativity that will man you down.

So, what if you are not here and can't get there? If you are not here at this moment, you cannot respond to the challenges or opportunities that are actually here. If your mind is constantly wandering in the past, then you won't be able to take action in the current moment or to create the life that you want. Meditation for men is a bicep-flex for your inner resolve and strength.

Step 1: Get a Timer.

You can download a meditation app using your device or you can use any timer you may have. You must pick a time and stick to it, don't move or stop until your timer stops too.

Step 2: Find the perfect comfortable place to sit.

Find a place so that you can sit with you back straight and upright. For a beginner, it is recommended the forward part of a chair so you're not slouching or leaning into the back.

Another option, you can have a few cushions on the ground so that your hips are higher than your knees when you sit cross-legged. Just think that your spine is a stack of blocks each resting on the other. Let your body structure hold you up. Your spine should be spine upright so that your attention can be on your practice and not the pain in your back.

Step 3: Set a time period.

Set your time period if how many minutes or hours you can do your session. You can start at 5 minutes that eventually increase the minutes each day. Make it impossible in which you will think you cannot follow but you will continue to push your edge.

Step 4: Eliminate distractions.

Turn off the phones and other gadgets and anything that will get for your attention and will cause you a distraction and will lose your focus and concentration.

Step 6: Set Your Focus.

It's important to have a solid focus point on your breath, the sensations in different areas of your body, a count of some sort. The methods that can keep you on your focus. Pick one and stick to it for the whole duration of the session and don't bounce around going from one method to another. Find the one that will work best for you and stick to it. There are a lot of methods and techniques, but these are the easiest to use in the beginning:

Follow Your Breath – find an area of your body like the inside of your nose or just where your breath moves in and out for your torso to focus. Through this method, you will be focusing on the sensation. What you have to do is to observe the sensations.

Counting Breaths - count your breath silently on your mind. This will help to quiet the brain.

Explore Your Body Sensations – pick a spot on your body that offers a sensation then just sit and feel the tingly energy moving around it.

Step 7: Start Your Session.

After doing all the steps above, that means you are doing good. You might get distracted but don't worry, stay on your mind and come back to your focus until your timer will stop.

Positive Thinking

The health benefits of positive thinking

Positive thinking may have an effect on our mental health. This might include:

- Increased life span
- Lower rates of depression
- Lower levels of distress
- Greater resistance to the common cold
- Psychological and physical well-being
- Cardiovascular health and reduced risk of death from cardiovascular disease
- Managing stress and times of difficulties properly

It is not yet scientifically proven why people who participate in positive thinking experience these health benefits. One concept is that when you have a positive outlook in life, it will allow you to survive better with stressful and depressing events.

Optimistic people tend to live their life healthier and happier as they indulge in physical activity, a healthier diet and not engaging in bad habits like drinking and smoking.

Focusing on positive thinking

Focus on your positive thoughts and do not entertain negative thinking. Your negative thoughts can turn to positive thoughts by thinking by applying the techniques below:

Classify parts that need to change.

If you want to be an optimistic person, classify the parts or areas on your life that you usually think negatively about, then work on that area. Divert them into more positive ways. Start small then focus on one area then the other.

Evaluate yourself.

Do a daily assessment and evaluation on yourself and your thoughts. If you that your thoughts are purely negative, then find a way to manoeuver those thoughts into a more positive and optimistic way.

Smile and laugh more often.

Find humor in everything especially when we are facing difficult times. Always put a smile on your face. Laugh often too. This will help you release the stress that you might be feeling.

Follow a healthier lifestyle.

Create a good exercise routine for yourself and aim to do these exercises for even at least 15-30 minutes daily. You can opt to cut out the minutes and do the exercise for 2 – 3 times a day. Keeping your body into movements can affect your mood and lesser stress. Follow a healthy diet for your body by planning your meals that you can still enjoy. Then manage stress properly.

Circle yourself with positive and cheery people.

If you surround yourself with negative people, it can only worsen your stress or any difficulties that you are dealing with. Instead, find a circle of people that can uplift you and support you on your dark days that can give you helpful advice.

Talk to your self positively.

Encourage yourself by saying positive things. If negative thoughts will come in your mind, veer them away and replace them with positive thoughts that you will think about yourself. Be grateful.

A Message for You...

Dear you,

You are kind. You put the well-being of others at the same level of importance as your own well-being. You place everyone's well-being at that level.

You are compassionate and you don't judge others. You seek to understand them, even if your point of view doesn't match yours. You accept them as they are and you don't bully or threaten others.

You are gentle and you speak tender words. You have a calm mind and a loving hand.

You have a big heart because you take nothing or no one for granted. You are generous of yourself, and share what you have with others.

You are vulnerable. You do not fear your emotions, and you allow yourself to feel them fully. You express them freely, in a controlled manner, and without hurting others.

You are optimistic. When you are happy, you see what you have, not what you don't have. You see the possibilities, not the obstacles. You don't limit yourself and you as you are limitless.

You are a questioning person. You ask questions, instead of making assumptions. You ask questions to come to your own conclusions, instead of just following the crowd. You ask questions so you can keep on learning new things, instead of just reinforcing what you already know.

You are resilient. You worked hard to become the person that you are now. You always pick yourself up off the ground and carry on. You are resilient to whatever things are thrown at you, which is good because life always throws things at you.

You are your best self. You are not afraid of failure. You learn from everything that happens to you.

You are an unconditional person. You are living a life without conditions. You love without conditions. You choose to accept people and situations as they are, instead of wishing they were different. You never try to change people. You either accept them as they are, or you stay away from them.

You are a fully alive person. You experience life in all its glory. You see and think with greater clarity. You feel intensely. You fear less and love more. You wake up every day looking forward to the day ahead. You go to sleep every night grateful for the day you had.

You are a fun-loving person. Happiness and fun go hand in hand. You see more opportunities for fun and you look at the world with wonder, and not in fear.

You are a patient person. You don't force things. You know everything unfolds in its own time. Sometimes that's fast, sometimes it's not.

You are a person with dreams. You know how you want to live, and are working towards that. Your dreams are not just dreams. They are your personal goals. And you take action.

You are a creative person. You tap into that part of you that exists in us all and find a way of expressing it. It doesn't matter how you express your creativity. You do it because it makes you happy and fulfilled to do so.

You are an in-the-moment person. You don't spend your time dwelling on the past or wishing for the future.

And you are a happy **YOU**.

I just want to give a big thank you to my biggest supporters.

To my amazing family: *Muriel (Mother), Shane (Brother), and Flo (Sister-in-law) – Thank you.*

To my work friends that are always there to listen: *Rachel, Colleen, Susan, and Cara – Thank you.*

To my four cats that give me joy on bad days: *Summer, Junior, Littler, and Leia – Thank you.*

To my boyfriend; *who has been my rock and biggest supporter for the past two years, Aaron – Thank you for being understanding and patient.*